Some Politically Incorrect Ideas©

Which road is for you?

The road less traveled?

This workbook is for you!

Bill Holley

Copyright © 2024 by The First Amended and Restated Holley Trust

All rights reserved. This book or any portion thereof may not be reproduced or used in any manner whatsoever without the express written permission of the publisher except for the use of brief quotations in a book review.
Printed in the United States of America
First Printing, 2024

ISBN: 978-1-917636-82-7 (Ebook)
ISBN: 978-1-917636-83-4 (Paperback)

Contact author at billholley11@yahoo.com

"If you're a person who is receptive to ideas that may stretch your mind a bit, this is a book for you"

"This is a workbook, not a novel. It is intended to present some ideas that may cause you to think about things a bit differently, and to give you a chance to put your thoughts on paper. A good way to do that is to read one idea a day, take time to think about that idea, and record your thoughts about it."

Contents

Politically Incorrect Idea #1 1

Politically Incorrect Idea #2 2

Politically Incorrect Idea #3 4

Politically Incorrect Idea #4 5

Politically Incorrect Idea #5 7

Politically Incorrect Idea #6 8

Politically Incorrect Idea #7 10

Politically Incorrect Idea #8 11

Politically Incorrect Idea #9 13

Politically Incorrect Idea #10 15

Politically Incorrect Idea #11 16

Politically Incorrect Idea #12 17

Politically Incorrect Idea #13 18

Politically Incorrect Idea #14 21

Politically Incorrect Idea #15 22

Politically Incorrect Idea #16 23

Politically Incorrect Idea #17 25

Politically Incorrect Idea #18 26

Politically Incorrect Idea #19 28

Politically Incorrect Idea #20 30

Politically Incorrect Idea #21 32

Politically Incorrect Idea #22 33

Politically Incorrect Idea #23 35

Politically Incorrect Idea #24 36

Politically Incorrect Idea #25 37

Politically Incorrect Idea #26 39

Politically Incorrect Idea #27 40

Politically Incorrect Idea #28 43

Politically Incorrect Idea #29 44

Politically Incorrect Idea #30 46

Politically Incorrect Idea #1

A white American can never fully understand what it's like to be black and can never fully understand what it was like to be a slave. Some of us might be able to understand intellectually. None of us can understand emotionally. The best we can do is to acknowledge the evils of slavery, acknowledge the more recent denial of civil rights to black Americans, and vow to do better. Most of us would like to do what we can to heal the wounds caused by those things and to move together toward a better future for all of us. As a German architect said, "The devil is in the details." How do we do that? It may be as simple and as complex as black Americans internalizing the idea that we can't change the past and that we've been making a good-faith effort for many years.

What do you think? _____

_____

_____

_____

Why do you think that? _____

_____

_____

_____

Politically Incorrect Idea #2

There's an article about racial reparations in the current issue of a national magazine. It seems reparations are simple: paying money to the descendants of slaves. The idea is simple, it is the details that aren't simple:

- Who should pay reparations, and how much should they pay?
- How far back should we go to determine who should pay?

Europeans and Asians made slaves of their own people back to Biblical times. Beginning about 500 AD and going on until about 1700 AD, Europeans were captured and transported to North Africa. Would the descendants of those people be paid reparations? Who else might qualify for reparations?

The slave trade from Africa to the New World started about 1525 and continued until about 1865. About 10,700,000 slaves were brought to the New World, about 380,000 of them to what is now the USA. If we consider only the USA, we still have difficult questions to answer.

- Should only blacks be paid reparations?

- If those who bought slaves and kept them in chains should pay reparations, shouldn't those who fought and died to free them from slavery and from their chains receive reparations?

- Who should pay reparations to the citizens whose ancestors died or were injured in the war to end slavery?

- Would it be our black citizens?
- How would the reparations paid to the descendants of slaves compare to the reparations of the descendants of those killed or wounded in the war to end slavery?

What do you think? _____
_____
_____
_____

Why do you think that? _____

_____

_____

_____

Politically Incorrect Idea #3

Enlightenment comes in strange ways. I was recently thinking about food allergies, about the craving for foods that are toxic to us, and about the strange power those cravings have. That's when I had one of those "aha" moments.

- What if the same thing that is true of foods is also true of relationships?
- What if the relationships we feel compelled to work at hardest, the ones that demand the most, the ones that give us the least, are the ones that are toxic to us?

Do you have relationships like that? _____

_____

What are you going to do about it? _____

Politically Incorrect Idea #4

There are many on college campuses who are now demonstrating in favor of Hamas because they see the Palestinians as being oppressed by Israel.

A bit of history might be worthwhile:

The first inhabitants of Palestine were the Canaanites, Semitic people. The first step in the process that created Israel began in 1917 when Britain said, in the Balfour Declaration, that it supported "the establishment in Palestine of a national home for the Jewish people" in the area it then controlled.

On November 29, 1947, the UN adopted Resolution 181, The Partition Resolution that divided Britain's Palestinian Mandate into Jewish and Arab states as of May 1948. In accordance with that resolution, David Ben-Gurion declared the sovereign state of Israel to exist on May 14, 1948. The USA immediately recognized Israel. It's worth noting that the UN actions did not establish a state of Palestine, and there is still no state of Palestine.

Palestine is a city, not a state or nation, and Palestinians are people who live in the city of Palestine. In the 76 years since Israel became a sovereign state, there have been wars between the Jews and the Arabs. The most recent was the surprise attack by Hamas, which is a Palestinian Sunni Islamist movement that governs part of the Gaza Strip, on October 7, 2023, that killed over 1,000 Israelis and took 253 hostages.

What do you think about what's happening in Gaza? _____

_____

_____

_____

Why do you think that? _____

_____

Politically Incorrect Idea #5

Muslims say we shouldn't judge all Muslims by the actions of a radical few, yet they don't distance themselves from those few. Is it fair to say they support the radical few by their silence?

We might want to consider the thoughts in a quote from the great British statesman Winston Churchill, who said, *"How dreadful are the curses which Mohammedanism lays on its votaries. Besides the fanatical frenzy, which is as dangerous in a man as hydrophobia in a dog, there is this fearful, fatalistic apathy. The effects are apparent in many countries: improvident habits, slovenly systems of agriculture, sluggish methods of commerce, and insecurity of property exist wherever the followers of the Prophet rule or live. A degraded sensualism deprives this life of its grace and refinement, the next of its dignity and sanctity. In Mohammedan law, every woman must belong to some man as his property, either as a child, a wife, or a concubine. They must delay the final extinction of slavery until the faith of Islam has ceased to be a great power among men. Individual Muslims may show splendid qualities, but the influence of the religion paralyzes the social development of those who follow it."*

Maybe we should treat Muslims differently.

What do you think? _____

_____

_____

_____

Why do you think that? _____

_____

_____

_____

Politically Incorrect Idea #6

There are several black Americans who have been very successful, but they lack leadership qualities that might allow them to lead the black community toward a peaceful nation, like Martin Luther King's vision.

Lacking that leadership, it is no surprise that the leadership that rises to deal with specific events is not the leadership that has a vision that stretches into the future, but the leadership of the loudest, leadership that focuses on the immediate, and leadership that incites violence. Unless that changes, we can expect more racial animosity, more violence, and a fractured nation that's sliding toward being a third-world nation.

What do you think? _____

_____

_____

_____

Why do you think that? _____

_____

_____

_____

Politically Incorrect Idea #7

The closing of a Walgreens store in Boston caused Ms. Ayanna Pressley, a member of Congress, to say it was racially motivated since the neighborhood is 85% black and Hispanic.

She also lamented the increased cost to residents of the area of essentials like baby food and diapers. She was right about that. The cost of those things will increase.

Either residents will have to travel farther to buy those things or buy from the smaller stores that have higher prices. Higher prices because they will incur the same costs related to theft, and will pass along to their customers those increased costs if they are to stay in business. In either case, essentials will cost more. In some cases, the residents will be unable to pay the increased costs and will change from being the working poor to living in poverty, unable to afford some of the essentials.

The government has long said that poverty creates crime, but Dr. Thomas Sowell, a noted economist, said, "It's the other way, that crime creates poverty," and it seems he is right. Crime, the theft that drove Walgreens out of the neighborhood, was the cause of the higher prices residents had to pay, and the higher prices drove some of them into poverty.

What do you think? _____

_____

_____

_____

Why do you think that? _____

_____

_____

_____

Politically Incorrect Idea #8

Why do so many black Americans identify themselves as African first and American second?

In the book *The Art of Losing*, a third-generation French woman goes back to Algeria, the homeland of her grandfather, and finds that the reality there is far different from the life she had in France and very different from the life she had imagined she would have in Africa. The role of women had changed little from when her grandfather lived there. Most of the people still lived in poverty. Women's rights were many years behind what she enjoyed in France. She, with her more modern view of women's rights, with easy access to all the necessities of life, and accustomed to a life with more equality with men, was not comfortable in the homeland of her grandfather. She just didn't fit in. Many of the things she took for granted in France were not available to her in Algeria.

If black Americans were to go to the Africa of their dreams, might they find the same thing that she did? To which country would they go? Might their experience be the same as the experience of the French woman?

What do you think? _____

_____

_____

_____

Why do you think that? _____

_____

_____

_____

Politically Incorrect Idea #9

A recent article talked about how unfair our society is to young black males who have a criminal record. It went on to talk about how unfair it is that their criminal record limits the opportunities those young men have. The article concluded that something is broken in our society, or that wouldn't happen. It made it seem as though their criminal records were totally independent of any wrongdoing, as though society gifted them with a criminal record as part of the process of growing from childhood to young adulthood. It would have been easy to read that and believe it, but there are a couple of things that should be considered, instead of accepting that, whole and entire.

Everything about race relations in the last many years is based on the unspoken assumption that blacks and whites are absolutely and totally equal in every way. But sociologists have long known that the environment influences our standards, our way of dealing with the day-to-day events of our lives, and our way of dealing with the adversities of life and the opportunities of life. Many poor youths, including many black youths, spend their childhood in an environment in which they are encouraged:

- to perpetuate the social responsibility, or lack of social responsibility, of their elders.
- to view the world as hostile, as lacking in opportunity.
- to view with suspicion any attempt to get them to better themselves in order to equip themselves with the knowledge that they need to be able to compete in a global economy.

Is that one of the reasons the poor stay poor, regardless of race?

What do you think? _____

_____

_____

_____

Why do you think that? _____

_____

_____

_____

Politically Incorrect Idea #10

Africa north of the Sahara is very different from Africa south of the Sahara. Per capita income is a pretty good indicator of the standard of living of the people.

- North of the Sahara, the per capita income ranges from $595 in Niger to $3,630 in Algeria
- South of the Sahara, per capita income is about twice as much, up to $7,337 in Botswana.

Might black Americans, who seem to almost worship all things African, have a different opinion if they knew more about Africa?

What do you think? _____

_____

_____

_____

Why do you think that? _____

_____

_____

Politically Incorrect Idea #11

How did we become a nation that embraces the negatives and ignores the positives? The negative bias of the media is obvious. If it bleeds, it leads is a pretty good description of the mindset of people who choose what we read and what we see on TV.

We don't, however, expect that of our universities, but they also embrace the negative. A study published by Rutgers University in 2019 said police use of fatal force is a leading cause of death of black men. If you read the study, you found that cops killing black men was the sixth cause of their deaths. Black men killing other black men was number three and was about three times number six.

The headline was misleading, and it distorted the facts. Why?

What do you think? _____

Why do you think that? _____

_____

_____

_____

Politically Incorrect Idea #12

After 9/11, there was a lot of press that said we should not hold Muslims accountable for the actions of a few Muslim extremists. Most of us agreed with that. However, we do hold large groups of people responsible for the actions of a few of a group's members. We gather all gun owners into a group, and hold the entire group responsible when one individual uses a gun to commit some atrocious act. We lump together all rednecks as being ignorant, anti-social, and worse. We label politicians as greedy, self-centered people who forget their constituents once they are elected. We even assume all whites are racist when a white is involved in an incident with a black.

Why do we give Muslims a free pass, when we aren't as understanding about other groups?

What do you think? _____

_____

_____

_____

Why do you think that? _____

_____

_____

_____

Politically Incorrect Idea #13

If a senior politician were to ask you to tell him what he should support in programs to help black Americans, to move the nation toward a more peaceful and unified society, what would you tell him?

- Would you talk about Diversity, Equity, and Inclusion (DEI), and about Critical Race Theory (CRT)?
- Would that bring our nation together?

Diversity, as defined by the government, means recognizing and respecting the uniqueness of each person.

Equity means that everyone has access to the same opportunity.

Inclusion occurs when everyone feels valued and included in group efforts.

No one can argue with those ideas. The problem is in the details of real-life situations.

- Where does diversity end?
- What is enough?
- If 12.1% of us are black Americans, as shown in the 2020 census, is one in eight (12.5%) enough, or is some higher number necessary?

TV ads now have enough blacks to make one believe that about 40% of us are black. The popular game show, Wheel of Fortune, has three contestants, and there is one black contestant almost every day.

Equity seems to have morphed from meaning equality of opportunity to equality of outcomes. Inclusion seems to mean that any group must have in it someone from every ethnic group, except whites.

White Americans can be under-represented without complaint. CRT is supposed to be a way of understanding how racism has shaped public policy. Note the past tense.

Is what was true in the past still true today? Does racism, a bias against black people, still shape public policy? It depends on where you look. In the federal government, 18.2% of employees are black. If public policy was racist, one would expect it would be evident where public policy is made, the federal government, but it isn't.

What do you think? _____

_____

_____

Why do you think that? _____

_____

_____

Politically Incorrect Idea #14

Research has shown that first-born children have a higher IQ and are over-represented as the top achievers in most things.

Does that mean that children born later are less smart and less likely to succeed? If so, then children in large families are more likely to be under-achievers, people who need help with the essentials in this high-tech world.

What families are most likely to have many children? Poor families that have little, or no, access to sex education and to birth control. That describes most of Africa. Is lack of birth control and large families one reason the people in places like Africa are so poor?

What do you think? _____

_____

_____

_____

Why do you think that? _____

_____

Politically Incorrect Idea #15

If you were asked to name the black leadership of today, what would you say? Could you name someone like Rev. Dr. Martin Luther King, Jr., or Rev. Ralph Abernathy? Could Rev. Jesse Jackson, Rev. Al Sharpton, or Rev. Henry Lyons fill those shoes? Could Barack Obama or Kamala Harris speak for black Americans? How about the founders of Black Lives Matter?

None of them seemed to want to be the leader of the black Americans, and none of them seemed qualified for that role. It seemed that Lt Col Allen West USA (Ret) might be that person. He's very smart, well educated, handsome, and a good public speaker. After two years in the House of Representatives and two years as the chairman of the Republican Party in Texas, he faded from public view.

Now Senator Tim Scott (R-SC) is the only person with any promise of becoming a national leader of the black community. He's also smart, handsome, and a good public speaker. In an interview with the Association of Mature American Citizens (AMAC), he was focused on the present and the future, not the past, and he seemed to be receptive to the ideas of others, things that might make him a good leader.

Is there another person who might become the leader of the black community?

What do you think? _____

_____

_____

_____

Why do you think that? _____

_____

_____

_____

Politically Incorrect Idea #16

Where did the trend toward our society treating men and women exactly the same begin? Might it have been in sports, when women sports reporters demanded to be allowed into men's locker rooms after games?

A federal judge then ruled that women could not be barred from men's locker rooms and the NFL issued an equal access rule that required every team to allow men and women equal access to locker rooms. Was that the beginning of the insistence that men and women are the same?

What do you think? _____

_____

_____

_____

Why do you think that? _____

_____

_____

_____

Politically Incorrect Idea #17

There is a lot of media coverage now about equality. To treat everyone the same, regardless of differences. We insist that men and women are exactly the same, despite obvious differences:

- We insist that transsexuals be treated exactly the same as those of us who didn't have "identity confirming" surgery.
- We insist that black Americans and white Americans are identical.

The government insists that everyone comply with the ideas of DEI, that we go along with the current thinking of others, and that we accept the idea that we're all equal in every way. It's not acceptable to encourage people to be different. When it's unacceptable to recognize individual accomplishment, to honor our ancestors, and to have an opinion that isn't popular in the media, it's refreshing to come across this comment by Marian L. Tupy, who's the editor of Humanprogress.org and a senior policy analyst at the Center for Global Liberty and Prosperity. He specializes in globalization, global well-being, and the political economy of Europe and sub-Saharan Africa. He said, "Progress depends on the flourishing of the talented. That means that inequality is truly the midwife of progress."

If he's right, what do you think our future will be like?

_____

_____

_____

Why do you think that? _____

_____

_____

_____

Politically Incorrect Idea #18

Blacks who are very successful seem as likely as underachieving blacks to point to the current social system and blame it for any perceived lack of success.

- Denzel Washington, who is a great actor, was quoted as saying, "If I was white, I'd be bigger than Paul Newman by now."
- Oprah Winfrey talks in unguarded moments about the disparity between white society and black society and

seems to believe the only reason for the disparity is racism.

- Rev. Henry Lyons, who was a great religious leader, said had he been white no one would have cared that he had a mistress, and that his wife tried to burn down the home he shared with his mistress.

Blacks who have achieved success in the existing system, who have been very successful financially, who have achieved fame, who have all things, tangible and intangible, to which most of us aspire, still point to racism as the reason they haven't achieved greater success.

What will it take to make blacks who are very successful stop blaming racism for not having even greater success?

What do you think? _____

_____

_____

_____

Why do you think that? _____

_____

_____

Politically Incorrect Idea #19

It seems many of us want a simpler life. They want to live as their ancestors did, to live more in tune with nature, to have more leisure time, and to get away from the stresses of modern life. If they could go back, they would find:

- that life was harsh
- that they had to work from sunrise to sunset to survive
- that there was little social life for people outside the cities
- that the average person was worn out from hard and unrelenting work by the time they were in their late forties
- that health care was crude by today's standards.

Given that, how many Americans would be willing to give up what we have today to go back to an earlier time:

- a time when you grew your own food or went hungry
- a time of hard and unrelenting labor
- a time without so many of the amenities we now enjoy

Today is a good time to be alive. We now enjoy a life that is much better than the lives of our ancestors and is much better than the lives of the people in most other countries.

What do you think? _____

_____

_____

_____

Why do you think that? _____

_____

_____

_____

Politically Incorrect Idea #20

A recent article said college enrollment is down for the first time in over 50 years. Why?

It's obvious that most jobs that pay well are either:

- in health care, where education is crucial
- in information technology, which also requires a lot of education

Do people no longer value a good job, one that provides a comfortable standard of living, or do many of our citizens now believe they will be provided with all they need without working?

If they think they won't have to work, that suggests that the change is linked to an entitlement mentality, a result of government programs that give everyone food, shelter, healthcare, and much more. Is it possible that those programs, started with the best of intentions, will ultimately lead to the end of our society as we know it, as fewer and fewer people are willing to spend years acquiring the skills and the knowledge that in the past made them self-supporting, that made them productive members of our society?

As the workforce shrinks, and the welfare society grows, there must come a time when our society is no longer self-sustaining, a time when what we produce is insufficient to satisfy the demands of our population.

How can we define that moment?

If we pass that moment, is there any way to reverse the trend and become self-sustaining again?

What do you think? _____

_____

_____

_____

Why do you think that? _____

_____

_____

_____

Politically Incorrect Idea #21

We have a crisis that threatens our border states with an influx of illegal immigrants that will swamp their welfare systems and change the very fabric of our society.

Part of the problem is that we've allowed our concern for human rights to adversely affect our legal system. An illegal who is female and has children is treated differently from a lone male. Why?

One of the bulwarks of our society is that everyone is presumed to be equal in the law. There's a lot of press about separating illegals who are mothers from their children, with calls for more humane treatment of them.

Consider this. A mother who's a citizen and who's broken the law, and is taken into police custody, will not keep her children with her. They will either live with relatives or be cared for by Child Services.

Why should we grant to illegals, women who've broken the law by entering this country illegally, rights we deny our own citizens?

To separate any mother from her children is a sad, but sometimes necessary thing.

What do you think? _____

_____

_____

_____

Why do you think that? _____

_____

_____

_____

Politically Incorrect Idea #22

The death of George Floyd, Jr. was a tragedy, as is the violent death of anyone.

It was assumed to be a hate crime, fueled by racism, and it caused widespread rioting. Would the cops have acted differently if the arrestee had been white, had been so violent it had taken four cops to subdue him? No one knows for sure.

Were the jurors in the trial of the four cops aware of the extent of the destruction that followed George Floyd, Jr.'s death? Did that knowledge influence their decision? No one knows for sure.

Would it have been better for our country if there had been a black leader who could have calmed the situation and led us to a non-violent solution?

What do you think? _____

_____

_____

_____

Why do you think that? _____

_____

_____

_____

Politically Incorrect Idea #23

There are many other instances of assuming something is caused by racism. Are they all right? Maybe looking at some facts will be illuminating.

- Since 1994, there has been no year in which the poverty rate of black married-couple families has been as high as 10%.
- There's been no year in which the national poverty rate has been as low as 10%.

What does that mean? Married black Americans aren't as poor as other black families and aren't as poor as most white Americans.

How could those things be true in a society in which racism is common?

Is it possible that much of what's attributed to racism is instead caused by other things?

What do you think? _____
_____
_____
_____

Why do you think that? _____

_____

_____

_____

Politically Incorrect Idea #24

There are many instances of assuming something is caused by racism. Are they right? Maybe looking at some facts will be illuminating.

It's assumed that the reason Africa is poor is the exploitation of Africa by whites. Is that true?

A Harvard study found that places in the temperate zone and located within 100 kilometers of the sea, were 8% of the world's inhabited land mass, but they had 23% of the population and 53% of the world's Gross Domestic Product.

Port cities flourished and non-port cities didn't. Africa, more than twice as big as Europe, has more coastline than Europe, and it has fewer seaports, 100 in Africa and 1,200 in Europe. Does that mean that geography is one reason Africa is so poor?

What do you think? _____

_____

_____

_____

Why do you think that? _____

_____

_____

_____

Politically Incorrect Idea #25

Is Islam a benign religion?

Consider this: Utility patent applications, new and unique ideas that lead to something better, are a pretty good measure of the intellectual freedom of a country.

- In 2022, the USA had 418,123 utility patent applications.

- Saudi Arabia, the biggest and the fourth-wealthiest country in Arabia, had 5,019.
- The USA has religious freedom.
- Saudi Arabia does not. It does have Islam as the dominant religion.

Does Islam discourage independent thought?

What do you think? _____

_____
_____
_____

Why do you think that? _____

_____
_____
_____

Politically Incorrect Idea #26

Pres. Joe Biden has signaled the end of this country as a meritocracy, a system based on performance, a system that evaluates and values someone based on what that person can do.

He said he would name a black woman to the Supreme Court, a position that requires a law degree.

- Bing.com says we have 1,300,000 lawyers.
- The American Bar Association says five percent of lawyers are black, so there are 65,000 black lawyers.
- Bing.com said 30% of black lawyers are female, so there are 19,500 of them.
- To be considered for the Supreme Court, a candidate should have distinguished herself in some way, maybe by becoming a partner in a law firm or becoming a tenured professor in a university.
- How many of the 19,500 would have done that, maybe at most a third, 6,500?

Is it racist to ask whether the best candidate would be one among that 6,500 or one among the other 1,293,500 lawyers?

What do you think? _____

_____

Why do you think that? _____

_____

_____
_____

Politically Incorrect Idea #27

It's become fashionable of late to speak in disparaging terms of prominent figures from our past as "old white men," minimizing their importance in our history. Are they worthy of respect, or do they deserve to be relegated to the dustbin of history?

Many of the early settlers, immigrants who had survived the dangerous crossing of the Atlantic Ocean in small boats, did not survive. They died from hunger and disease. The best available estimates put the number who either died or returned to Europe as high as 50%. Life was tough in those days. Should we ignore that part of our history? Should we disparage those brave men and women who sailed to an unknown new world in search of a better life for themselves, a life that did not have royalty with inherited titles, a life that promised more to those who were willing to work hard and to adapt to the reality of a different land?

When the 56 signers of the Declaration of Independence said, "They pledged their lives, their fortunes, and their sacred honor," that was literally true. They knew the British would consider what they did high treason, punishable by death. Britain was a world power then, with an unequaled navy and an empire that girdled the globe. They were proud that "the sun never set on the British empire." An impartial observer would have given the colonies little chance of succeeding, yet those men were willing to die to create a new nation, where there was no royalty and where every man had a chance to be whatever he dreamed of being. Nine died fighting the British. Should their bravery be rewarded by being labeled "old white men" and spoken of in derogatory terms?

The Civil War lasted from 1861 to 1865 and cost the nation over 600,000 deaths and over 900,000 injured, some crippled and unable to work, plus about $1,500,000,000,000 in property loss. Using a modest inflation number of 3%, that's about $5,835,000,000,000 in today's money. Virtually all the killed and injured were white. They fought to preserve the nation and to end slavery. Were those warriors, who fought to liberate black Americans, "old white men" only worthy of being spoken of in terms that range from denial of their sacrifices to terms that can be described, at best, as disrespectful?

Those people were just like us in many ways. Like us, they sometimes fell short of their own expectations, and far short of what we now demand of our heroes, but their positive achievements were monumental. They lived in times very different from what we have now. Are they just "old white men" who deserve no honor, or were they true heroes, by the standards of the times in which they lived or any other time?

What do you think? _____

_____

_____

_____

Why do you think that? _____

_____

_____

_____

Politically Incorrect Idea #28

Some blacks being racist would explain much of what is happening today, but that's not an acceptable idea in our politically correct society. One who dares to voice such an idea is told he's blaming the victim, or worse. To be socially accepted, one must never depart from what's communally accepted, even if common sense suggests the accepted ideas aren't the only ones that may be possible. That limits the use of language.

Dr. Edmond Land, the developer of the first instant camera, said "a problem well defined is half solved". If we can't even define the problem without being severely hampered by limits imposed by what's acceptable language, how are we to ever solve the problems of race in this country?

We must either take a new and different look at race relations, without being limited, as we are now, or we must expect that race relations will get worse, despite our best intentions and our best efforts to create a society in which everyone is treated like a valuable person. What is a good first step in working toward better race relations?

What do you think? _____
_____
_____

Why do you think that? _____

_____

_____

_____

Politically Incorrect Idea #29

It seems that the only thing white Americans and black Americans agree on is that white Americans should have done more in the past, should do more now, and should do more in the future, to atone for slavery and segregation. What more should we have done in the past?

White Americans suffered the loss of over 600,000 men killed, over 900,000 wounded, and much destruction of property in the war that ended slavery.

To our shame, nothing much happened from the end of that war until 1954, when the Supreme Court ruled that segregated schools were unconstitutional. Then, we began to make some progress in efforts toward equal rights for everyone.

- The Civil Rights Act of 1957 protected the voting rights of everyone, including black Americans.
- Executive order 10925, signed into law March 6, 1961, required government contractors to "take affirmative action to ensure that applicants are employed and that employees are treated during employment without regard to their race, creed, color, or national origin".
- The Civil Rights Act of 1964 banned segregation on the grounds of race, religion, or national origin in all public places. Rev Dr Martin Luther King, Jr. called it "a second emancipation."
- The Voting Rights Act of 1965 outlawed any attempt by states or cities to keep black Americans from voting.
- The Fair Housing Act of 1968 made it illegal to deny someone housing based on race.
- The Equal Employment Act of 1972 made it illegal for an employer, union, or employment agency to discriminate against an applicant or employee due to a person's race, color, religion, sex (including pregnancy, gender identity, and sexual orientation), national origin, age (40 or older), disability, or genetic information (including family medical history).
- In 1979, the Equal Employment Opportunity Commission (EEOC) became responsible for handling all claims of employment discrimination.

We spent the next thirty years trying to make the intent of those laws an everyday fact of life. In 2009, The Hate Crimes Prevention Act became law. What more, specifically, should we have done?

What do you think? _____

_____

_____

_____

Why do you think that? _____

_____

_____

_____

Politically Incorrect Idea #30

It seems that corporate America is now the target of a lot of negative press. There's a lot about corporate greed, a lot about corporations not paying their fair share of taxes, and a lot about income inequality. It's easy to believe that there are no benefits to having corporations operate in a free enterprise environment.

- There's nothing about corporations that fail to compete and go out of business.

- There's nothing about the availability of consumer goods at prices that happen because of competition in a free market.
- There's nothing about the positives and a lot about the negatives of the system we have.

One example of the benefits we enjoy because of free enterprise and competition is the hand-held calculator. A Japanese company produced the first one, with the basic four math functions, in 1970. In 1971, the TI-2500, sold by Texas Instruments, cost $149.95. It was profitable, so other companies began to produce hand-held calculators. Now, a calculator with those four functions, plus four others, is for sale online for $5.49. Why did that happen? Was it some government program, or was it competition among corporations in a free market that brought the price down so much? Was the public well served by those corporations?

What do you think? _____

_____

_____

_____

Why do you think that? _____

_____

Roots of an Oak tree

Can you see it more clearly now?
That's what this book does – help you
see more clearly

This book is in black and white.
The ideas in it are NOT!

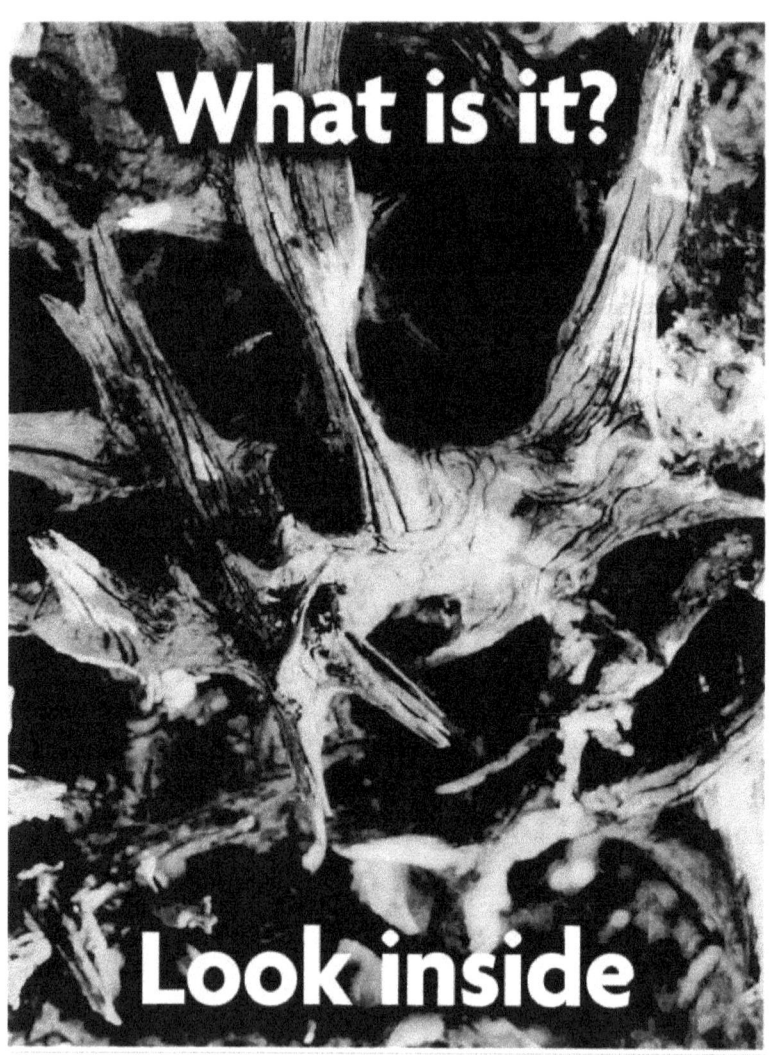